GAU-TRAINED

POEMS & STORIES

GAU-TRAINED

POEMS & STORIES

FLOW WELLINGTON

Self-Published through Poetree Publications (Pty) Ltd, 2018

Poetree Publications (Pty) Ltd
PO Box 545, Sunninghill
Johannesburg
www.facebook.com/poetreepub
poetflow@live.com

Printed and bound in Johannesburg, South Africa
Editing and proofreading: Poetree Publications & HoBEC
Cover Design: Shruti K (India)
Photography: Kim Murison & Rolland Motaung
Typesetting: Eurobook 70gsm, Calibri 10pt

ISBN 978-0-9946950-2-4 (paperback)
First Edition

Dedicated to the brave, the forgotten and the persevering.

"The truth isn't always beauty, but the hunger for it is."
– Nadine Gordimer

Contents

Acknowledgements

The beginning: to Ilze Maya and Neasah Swarts for opening their hearts and home to me when life had chewed me up and was ready to spit me out onto the grimy streets of poverty. Thank you for nursing me back to health (physically and emotionally) – and for the black couch I slept, worked, ate on for a year - I love you forever!

The middle: to every individual or collective group who saw me worthy and trusted me to handle their publishing projects, and creating a part of their legacy. I will always be grateful and acknowledge the role my clients play in pushing me forward. Your faith in my capabilities has fuelled and propelled me to pursue greater heights. Thank you!

The in-between: to my carefully chosen life-partner, Rolland Motaung; I leap and your love catches me every time. Thank you for faith, perseverance, patience and often, an unseen military fist that keeps pushing me to be better, do better and live better. Upward and onward!

The now: to everyone in the literary community who gave me hope and courage to write and share again; to friends who offer honest, strict critique and encouragement; to the ones who give writers a space to shine; and to everyone who believes literature is still a saviour in this word... You are seen, you are loved!

The unspoken: acknowledgement must be given to those who played a silent part in providing the content to this book – the homeless, the forgotten, the night crawlers, the bourgeois' and the paupers... every one living in and pushing their way through life in Jozi, I see you.

And to me: I've been forged in fire and here I am, sharper than ever and still standing!

Prologue

Relocating to Johannesburg was an easy decision. The months leading up to my day of departure from Port Elizabeth had been some of my most mentally and emotionally draining: my business venture had failed because of a friend's betrayal; I was broke and moping around my mother's house day after day. I had nothing, and nothing positive was happening. So I packed a suitcase, booked a bus ticket with some money I had made from cleaning houses and left my home town.

I had fooled myself into thinking that I'd only be in Joburg for a month: to record a poetry album. I didn't really know what I was getting myself into. I had never been to the city, I had only R100 in my pocket and I was still crazy in love with the guy I was going to visit. Sure enough, we picked up right where we left off, from the minute we saw each another on the Park Station platform, and things went downhill from there.

It wasn't easy to admit that I was trapped in an abusive relationship – I was oblivious and delusional. I was living in one of Africa's most vibrant cities but even after a year I had never been anywhere outside of Van Der Kloof Street, Ruimsig. I was withering away, physically and mentally. When I wrote some of the pieces like *Derailed*, *West Rand*, *Escape* and others, I kept thinking about other women in that situation. How many women follow some fiery love connection to an unknown place and end up isolated and destitute? I'd like to believe that women will find courage in the pages of this book, to recognise their circumstances and leave, no matter how desperate the situation or how dependent they think they are on the person. My situation pointed me in all the right directions once I walked away and chose life over love. I learned how to trust in honesty and brokenness, and that revealing the truth meant being true to yourself and that there was always another, better way.

Life in the City of Gold is not all roses and sunshine. So many people come here – from around the country and across borders – to find their wealth and success, to make it big, or just to make a better living than the one they had wherever they come from. Joburg will really show you flames if you're not careful. I didn't come here with a solid plan; and I fell flat on my face as a result of that. Sure, with the right connections and enough ambition and guts you can make a hell of a life here, but others (many) are not so fortunate. Living in the heart of the Jozi CBD showed me how sugar-coated our tourism campaigns are and how, even at the dinner table of a family in the rural areas, the dream is clothed in a shimmering coat of many colours.

Writing about the things I saw every day in this City and living through things that most people only see on the news – like witnessing mob justice over a petty crime or a drug deal going down at the brothel across the street – gave me a clear sense of what the average human has to endure every single day just to stay alive. In *Doctors without Borders*, *Sex & the City*, *City of Gold* and many pieces I included in the sections Derailed and Crossroads, I highlight what some would call the filth of Joburg. I felt, more than anything, to write these stories into the book, to give these people who battle through the worst living conditions in the CBD a voice, in some way. I'd like to think that one cannot say you *know* Jozi unless you've experienced this *real* Jozi: the crowded taxi ranks, the endless rows of hawkers, the dirty, dirty streets and the thugs lurking on every corner.

Among all this chaos are also the stories of the forgotten and forsaken and the genuinely innocent: families, brothers and sisters from neighbouring countries who seek refuge here (as told in *Borders*), the average Joe (and Jane) trying to make an honest living by selling *amagwinya* and grilled walkie-talkies on the streets, and the millennial who's climbing that proverbial ladder to make his/her family proud, by any means necessary. This city holds so much of everything for everyone! I thought about writing and including stories about the affluence and golden side of the city, or about the hashtags that have been in the forefront of our daily existence, but I was constantly drawn back to telling the stories of the most unspoken truths. For me, the content had to be as close to the real thing as possible because I lived it (especially topics on poverty (*Jeppe*), abuse (*Last Straw*), postnatal depression (*Runaway Train*) and race (*Mixed Enough* and *Afrika Kind*)), and because I have the resources to generate conversations about it. There was going to be no romanticising of anything in these pages.

As much as this book is a retrospective journey of my own life – from 2011 to 2017, mostly – it is also anyone's journey: from arriving in Johannesburg (The Platform), to the pushing and pulling that the city inadvertently does on you (Derailed and Crossroads), to the realisation that there is always hope and light when you reach out and push beyond your limits (Full Steam Ahead). I don't profess to be any sort of authority on the subject matter; for the most part, I experienced more privilege than I give credit to over the past six years, but I do know something about being penniless, homeless and desperate in this place, and I am a testament of how a woman can be victorious and powerful through the worst adversity. This offering was compiled with care, and consideration for who would pick it up and who would find the gem that would impact them.

May this book be a blessing to all who read it, and may it inspire you to keep moving onward and upward to reach your Higher Power.

Though based on realistic events, the poems and stories in this book are mostly fictional, including all names of key characters. Places and locations are mentioned in context, but are not necessarily the exact areas of any events or situations portrayed in this book.

THE
PLATFORM

THE CITY

Towering towers, rowdy roads –
  The City is in a class if its own.
Hurried hellos, cultivated clones –
  Both city slicker and street vendor call it home.

Bustling business, pending profits –
  The City churns a coin and paper element.
Bothering beggars, smouldering suits –
  In between, the average admits impediments.

The City sleeps with one eye open;
  Spying blatantly on night crawlers.
She is still… aware of the unspoken; her shadows hide –
  Her breathing drowns out the snickering prowlers.

She'll pounce when least expected,
  Have her way till she's had her fill;
Turn a blind eye, leave undetected –
  In the City nothing is free, not even your will.

Awake, she is fresh, oblivious;
  Welcoming the new dawn, the challenge.
The City holds no sentiments, uncommonly promiscuous –
  She leaves you clinging to memories: the beauty and the malice.

Alluring amusement, temporary temptations –
  The City holds an enchanting mystique.
Offers opportunity, diverse dimensions –
  The City speaks new language that leaves you weak.

Intense intensions, fabricated fulfilment –
  A place of an ever-changing tune.
Majestic madness, blissful bewilderment –
  The City is me, the City is you!

PARK STATION

Rows of tattered luggage
Queue between piles of worn-out passengers –
This one stacked for the seaside,
That, there, will try to cross another border;
The road is long and the boiled eggs are niffing.

Here arrives another busload of hopefuls
Chasing fool's gold and what-not.
They'll muster all their power to trek life-belongings
To some godforsaken 10th floor,
Then break their backs digging their dreams out of
The back of a Pikit Up truck.

Look how the Jozi sun smiles on them:
Rays of golden corn charring on every corner –
This is where you can make a killing
Just by killing time.
There's money dripping from the walls in this town;
You just need to know which platform to step onto.

Thousands of tired feet scuff their way around these floors:
Clutch the purse, the phone, the child's hand –
Everything is a bargaining chip
And finders-keepers is a winning game.
This is the port of entry where the rat race begins, and
If you make it out onto the streets above
You'd better tuck that naïve smile deep into your pockets;
Save it for the other side of the tracks.

These benches host business deals and
Family meetings all in one sitting;
Their arms are sticky, holding a toddler's drool,
Lovers' farewell tears and more often,
A homeless father's longing:

The busses come and go but
His kin will mourn him and close the case.

Welcome to the City of Gold:
Slide further down the rainbow...

KNOWING

About Love

I

your eyes hold a thousand secrets;
they drink up all my vulnerability and
drown my common sense.

II

your fingers trace the contours of my face,
teaching your palms how to steal my laughter
and hide my dreams between your lifelines.

III

your web of lies glistens
as you spin the sun's rays around my heart;
the occasional silver lining blinds the tangled mess.

knowing should save me.
knowing is not enough.

About family

IV

blood bonds break easily
when silence offers an escape route;
the truth is too thick to swallow.

V

absent fathers are blamed for the
mistakes of mistreating mothers, while
the Ancestors call lost children to an unknown home.

VI

the bitterness of your memory
swirls between my taste buds,
reminding me to spit and cleanse with every libation.

Knowing is a saviour.
Knowing is everything.

IGNORANCE IS BLISS

Kelly-Leigh lives in a revamped building in the Jo'burg CBD with her African boyfriend. I can't pronounce his name; they all sound the same to me. I don't see her too often but she sends me some money now and then. It's enough to keep her father quiet.

When she told us she was moving to Johannesburg Central to be closer to her work, I wasn't too happy. You hear so many stories about that place: drug lords, pimps, muggings on every corner. She told us she will be living in the better part of town, near Maboneng where the hipsters and cool, artsy people hang out. I suppose that makes it better if she's around culture and such. Her father thinks she's wasting her life away, 'living la vida loca' as he puts it. Kelly is a good girl though; brains and beauty. She's not like the girls she used to go to school with who got pregnant in Matric or dropped out because they were chasing taxi driver boyfriends. No, my Kels has a good head on her shoulders.

After she matriculated she went to varsity, you know. Studied Civil Engineering... or Quantity-something? I don't really remember but she wanted to work in *Gov'ment*. She also wanted to be a Promotions Manager at some stage. Leonie's sister got her a casual doing in-store activations for the holidays. I was glad she was making her own money. These kids want all sorts of luxuries that we can't always cater for. So its better that she bought her own things; taught her about independence. She liked that job *nogal*. Dressed up and did her makeup well every day. She said her supervisor was quite impressed with her; more than the other girls. A fast learner that Kelly... She was going places! We sort of had to understand later that she was struggling to find a job in her field of study. Things are hectic in South Africa, *mos*. She went on a lot of interviews for a long time but nothing concrete came up. So she's full time in the promotions business now; doing well for herself. This year it's going on two years and she's very stable, with a car and nice clothes and her own place, with her African boyfriend. My Kelly... all grown up.

Last Christmas, when my sister passed away, it was Kelly who paid for most of the funeral arrangements. Magda-and-them *mos* didn't have policies and such. Her husband was a mason in the country all these years. We all chipped in but Kelly and her boyfriend paid for the coffin and undertakers and all the catering. They even paid for a tent and chairs to put up in the yard. That's when I knew her father and I would be well taken care of in our old age. Even though she gives her father grey hairs with her extravagance and unorthodox manners, she's still his baby girl. He always says he doesn't want the money she sends if it's coming from that *darkie*, but secretly I know he's happy to be eating burger patties and the fancy Russian sausages every month. He could never stay angry at Kels for too long, anyway.

We were supposed to visit at her flat over the New Year. I was going to make potato salad and sandwiches with the left over Christmas gammon and tongue meat. We've never been there, even when she moved in a year ago. She said she wasn't ready to have people over because she was still decorating and making it homely. Only a mother would understand that, of course. I was actually quite disappointed when she said we had to cancel the get-together; apparently she was called in urgently to work because they were short-staffed. I'm hoping we can go there some time. I'd like to see where my baby is resting her head every night. And also maybe buy one of those multi-coloured African shirts that all the foreigners wear. It sounds exciting where Kelly lives; not at all like anything shown on the news. The only thing you see on TV about the CBD is murder, prostitution and Xenophobia. I hope that African boyfriend of hers looks after her. But he does seem like a nice boy, though, well-mannered and clean.

You know, sister Edna from church asked us to pray for her daughter last week in the prayer meeting. Apparently, she also lives in Jo'burg Central but in a rough area. Sister Edna says she hardly ever hears from her daughter anymore and only gets an eWallet of R1,000 once a month. Shame, I can only imagine how desperate sister Edna must feel not knowing where or what or how. At least I know Kelly-Leigh has a good job doing promotions and making good money.

Come to think of it, Kelly and that girl went to varsity together. They used to go to campus gatherings and hung out in the same crowd. Yes, I think there are some photos of them in Kelly's old room at home. Such a pity how things turn out for some people, hey? I'll have to ask Kelly if she knows anything about the girl's whereabouts.

WHISPER

a cool breeze softens my brow
and lifts my eyes towards the horizon.
from across the vast expansion I smell that salty whisper
that often sounds like home.

DERAILED
DERAILED

WHERE I'M FROM

Van Duuren Street:
An uphill stretch of old and new;
Familiar, but not quite the same anymore.
This was home – with nippy mornings
Filled with the aromas of shoe polish and mielie meal porridge
And the sweet melodies from a gramophone.
Here were uncles and brothers, fathers and friends
On corners and spaza shop verandas;
And Coltrane and Armstrong jamming with Ernie Smith
From generations of boom boxes.
In Van Duuren Street our bones grew to the major and minor scales
Of toilet roll trumpets, plastic crate pianos and coffee tin drums,
And Sundays we followed the brass band's tunes
All around the church yard.

What do these new layers of bricks and fresh paints
Know about the smell of homemade bread,
Cinnamon koeksisters and vetkoek with jam;
Where steamy kitchens were the breaths needed
For bugle horns and table tops provided a platform
For Theloneous Monk to serve a feast for the ears?
Ah, Van Duuren Street:
Where Oupa and his friends drank Old Brown Sherry
With Hugh Masekela and Abdullah Ibrahim in their cars,
And wished the Alabama still had smoky nights with
Their girls in red dresses swinging by the bandstand.
Old men wearing hats, mimicking those compositions –
This was my Sophiatown, my District 6,
My Bo Kaap, our new South End in the Northern suburbs,
Where strings held us together and piano chords
Gave us the keys to life.
It was groovy, where I'm from
But not quite the same anymore.

CONDITIONING

"Mother has lived a hard life," she said,
Lips smiling, eyes lying, heart burning;
Her chest always tightens when she is forced
To mention her still living birth portal –
Her name chokes in her throat and scorches her vocal chords.
"Mother worked hard to put us through school," she said,
Memories flooding, sensations numbing;
She knows very well that obligation does not equate to love
And bitterness sweetens the excuses and reasoning...

Mother is a hurricane: thrashing through concrete fortresses
And uprooting even the deepest assurances!
She is a storm that brews silently and bursts
The harshest of winds – her ominous scowls and
Thundering bellows are enough
to shatter
            the windows
                        to your soul,
So she can gust in and crumble
All the protective walls you've built.
"No, mother never really means the things she says," she said,
Teeth clenching, fists balling, head spinning;
She knows enough to understand that the deeper the wound
The longer it takes to heal, and broken bones
Never really walk the same way again...

Mother is a reminder: breathe stronger when walking over fiery coals;
Drink your tears when your heart begins to parch;
And blood is cleansed by oxygen;
so breathe...
            breathe and exhale
                        all the toxins of conditioning.

DRIVING MISS CRAZY

Too many smiles I've kept to myself,
Shared only in reflections, in secret moments.
Too many smiles I've forced: prescriptions meeting expectations;
I want for nothing; still, my needs are not met.

So many rivers I've cried, drowning in applause
And praise, swept away by current affairs.
So many rivers have dried: barren they flow;
Every day is an outer-body experience.

I'm holding *my* hand, carefully guiding my footsteps;
The circles I've walked around myself are broken rings
of stumbling blocks.
Even with the light on I lose my way,
But I see so clearly in the dark.

It's loud... loud in the silence of compressed sign language.
Like inaudible screams from a soundproofed mouth –
I'm a multi-lingual mime!

I have just this to offer you: nothing but my everything.
All of my volumes, pages drenched in my love potion of tears and
ink.
I will bleed my heart out in punct-u-a-tion, marking the words I am
so full-of... stop, to turn the page.

The best is yet to come
But I need just to feel the good, the better.
I want to need. I need to want.
To share the smiles in public moments.

DERAILED

I always imagined I'd spend my life
In a cabin with a wraparound veranda,
Off the coast of what-where
Or maybe among the rolling hills or countryside of here-there.
And I'd just write poems and stories…
Poems and stories about you:
You with your sheep's-wool hair, dark as the night;
Smile that covered half your face…
Poems and stories *for* you.

Instead, I am here: in the balconied room of someone else's house
Constantly tiptoeing around on borrowed time.
Here, where some nights I sleep on the bathroom floor
With the locked door standing guard over me,
My tears washing the cold tiles are my secret poems;
Secret poems and stories *about* you.

ESCAPE

I could squeeze through these bars if I tried hard enough. Tina was staring at the security gate that towered between her and the driveway.

It's been 3 days since her husband had left on his business trip and the food he had bought was almost done. Tina wasn't sure when he would return; sometimes he'd be gone for a week at a time and she'd have to ask the neighbour's kids to bring her some food on their way from school. She didn't want to wait for the bread to run out this time; she would not involve the children in her struggles again. *This lock could be jimmied with a pin, right; like in the movies?* She considered how resourceful she used to be when she lived on her own – things had changed so much.

When Tina met Zwandile, he had been a guest at a friend's house for a few months; they were working on a music project together. She was instantly taken by him: tall, dark, charming to both men and women. He wasn't exactly handsome, but his charisma gave him a glorious energy. They started dating almost immediately and in no time, they were caught up in an intense love affair. Between Zwandile's extensive traveling and Tina's devoted longing for him, they remained connected even when he was gone for months at a time. No one would have thought things could go sour between them... no one.

I could jump from the balcony and over the wall?! Her mind was racing through every scenario and option; none seemed completely doable, or safe for that matter. Jumping from the balcony was a huge risk: she could twist her ankle, or worse. Squeezing through the gate's bars was an even worse idea: what if she got stuck and he found her there when he got back? She was tempted to call on the neighbours for help but they all adored Zwandile. She doubted that they would help her. Most didn't even know she lived there.

This was her one shot. Tina was determined to escape from this prison she had called home for more than two years.

In the beginning, Zwandile was everything he had always been: loving, caring, considerate; Tina had everything she'd always wanted. He worked hard and they lived comfortably; she really couldn't complain. But there was one thing Tina knew about Zwandile that no one else did: he was an extremely jealous man with a very short temper. Tina had moved to Johannesburg to live with him after they had been an on-and-off item for two years, and within a few months she had gone from social and carefree to a bored recluse who wasn't even allowed outside without permission. Things were changing fast but she continued to make excuses for him, and even for her own transformation. In no time, Tina found herself spending nights locked in the bathroom and sleeping on the cold tiles. She was constantly walking on egg shells. If she spoke wrong, challenged his opinion or chatted to one of his friends he would dig into her with the harshest insults and tongue lashing. She feared him... resented his apparent love and affection.

Tina was hastily packing a bag; something small enough to carry only the bare necessities. She was going to attempt the balcony jump, no matter the cost. She had managed to convince herself that the drop was not that far and even if she did twist her ankle, the neighbours' wall was low enough to drag herself over – she was going to risk it all and hope for their sympathy. It was just about ten in the morning; there was no way Zwandile would get back at that time. *Why would he rush back, anyway?* she thought as she tossed the bag over the rails and onto the grass below. *It's now or never!*

*****

The clouds were starting to gather above her head; the chill in the air was creeping beneath her shirt, between her bones. It was dusk already; Tina could hear pots and cutlery clanging from next door: supper was being served. The pain had seeped all through her body and after all these hours, she felt like she had broken more than just her leg. Her agonising cries retired to hopeless whimpering: *why is no one coming to help me? What's wrong with people?* She tried to remember which day of the week it was. If it were Tuesday, the gardener would find her in the morning. He'd call an ambulance and she'd be free. But he'd most likely call Zwandile as well... Tina was dragging her numb body towards the side gate, hoping that someone would walk by and see her, hear her, help her.

It was dark and freezing when Tina's hand finally clutched the bottom of the wooden gate. She heaved a sigh of relief, drained and distressed. *I can make it*, she told herself and began calling out for help. She heard a faint tap coming from the kitchen window above her head. There was no one in the house so she ignored it; it must have been a bird or one of those hard-shelled insects. She called out again and this time the tapping was louder.
She looked up and there was Zwandile, glaring down at her from inside the house. He was home and that meant that she would not be going anywhere, anymore.

WEST RAND

Red sand
Quiet streets
Midnight walks
Hip hop beats

High walls
Racist fears
Student lives
Drugs and beers

Starlit skies
Balcony confessions
Pretending bodies
Keeping up appearance

Hungry bellies
Secret lives
Love destroyed
A foetus died.

BORDERS

I want to tell my father I've made it:
Off the farmlands;
Out of the streets;
Across the border to this City of Gold.

I want him to know that I've followed in his footsteps;
Come to make a better life –
Come to make Mama proud;
Come to find him and show him I am a man!

I want to ask my father if his travels went smoothly;
I want to ask him if it was all the magic he told us kids about?
Did he find a good job; did he make his fortune;
Did he remember us?

I want to tell him: Papa, I want to do better, be better;
Live better than the two-room mud house you raised us in.
I want to eat better, dress better and sleep softer.

I left the farmlands.
Abandoned our streets.
I stood, waiting my turn at the border: "Papers, please!"
I've come to his City of Gold to find him...

But they will tell my mother that it was a difficult situation.
They will send her what's left of me in a box, along with my papers
And they will tell her times were hard.

She will know that I sat in the corner of my shack, waiting:
Waiting for them to break in,
Waiting for it to be over.

She will see, in the papers, that an outsiders travels
Do not go smoothly

And gold is not meant for my complexion.

I wonder if crossing the border
Was everything my father had hoped it would be?

IMPEPHO

there's a candle, always burning,
in the window of the thatch-roofed house.
the drumming and the humming
send children scattering from its stoep –
this is the house of spirits, they say.

there is an old man, always hunching,
who loiters in the garden of this house.
he waits for darkness and a calling
from his master to fulfil unspeakable duty –
he is the boogieman they warn against.

there are the posters, so disturbing,
of the missing children of Hemel Valley.
they are littered and trampled through the streets –
they seem to always get stuck between the thatch.

there is a stench, most repulsive,
that the wind often picks up along its way.
it is familiar mixed with sinister;
leaves a sudden bloody taste, then drifts on –
and the candle keeps burning, scent of impepho lingering.

FIRE IN YOUR SCARS

Being a woman burns.
Between the ears,
Inside the chest
Between the thighs
It burns scars into silken flesh
And is dressed with Calamine and Herbal smiles

Speaking for the woman burns.
Slits tongues,
Rips hearts to shreds
Scorches throats
That try desperately to
Silence the rage.

And it cannot be named anything else but rage
Because fire does not tame
Even when the flames die down
There are red-hot coals in our bellies
And orange embers dancing around
In our mouths

Being a woman burns.
Sends regimes crumbling to ashes
And weakens the longevity
Of generational conformity
Womanhood burns in 3rd degrees
That refuse to be hidden by pretty skirts and makeup

We burn tattoos into our flesh
To honour our scars.

DOCTORS WITHOUT BORDERS

There's a blue door looming in an alley:
The sore thumb sticking out along the endless grey walls;
They all know the secret knock
And the best time to find the doctor in –
The waiting room is always full.

At least five floors of this building
Keep the Authorities' pockets full.
Single mums piggy-back snot-nosed kids
Up and down the bleached stairs to their two-roomed flats –
'Mommy has to work tonight'; they'll sit quietly in the hallway,
Waiting outside the door until Mr Officer has done his rounds.

Black arrows direct visitors to the sixth and seventh landings
Where cold stares and the stench of rotting blood greet you every time:
Turn left to Find Lost Lovers; turn right for all Enlargements.
Credentials are unimportant here; if the price is right,
There's a solution to your problem.

Behind closed doors there are often screams and moans
As un-gloved hands spread and probe.
Rusty tongs and pliers take care of delicate procedures
Which leave a lifetime of cuts and bruises –
The Medicine Man on the top floor will burn imphepo
And ask every Ancestor for the right remedy.

In the morning the blue door stays open
As bags of disease-dripping needles are dumped
On heaps of tiny, lifeless limbs: the alley reeks of pasts, presents and futures.
And the Doctors retreat to their lavish, North-side homes
Before the City comes knocking again.

SECOND FLOOR

Outside my window is a big tree
Where ruffed-up city pigeons sleep and
Sparrows' nests swing in the midnight breeze.
Outside my window are city lights,
And night club music;
And there are women screaming,
Beat down by drunken fists, who claim to love them,
Cut by the same bottlenecks that will stab someone
Around the corner for their small change,
For a blanket,
For *nje*...
Outside my window is a big tree
That shadows me as I watch helplessly every night –
Thanking my Ancestors that I am inside,
Behind this window.

SEX AND THE CITY (Pt 1)

By the time I turned 5 years old
I knew where each of the cracks in the paint start and end,
Here, against our wall outside the station.
When I am 10, I will know all the good corners around town
And Mama will show me how to count the coins in piles of 50.
At the age of 15 I will move to the big, grey building across the street
Where Mama spends most of her nights;
The grey building where the women are loud and
The men are drunk and it smells like the drain next to our wall.
When I live in the grey building I will get new, clean clothes
And new hair... and Mama will show me how to count
The paper money into piles of 200.
I'll have my own room, with my own bed and
Lots of visitors – Mama says I'm one of the pretty ones;
And it won't be all bad: sometimes it will be nice
Because some of the men smell nice and talk nice –
I must practice being nice, too.
But I am not yet 15; only Mama can go to the grey building.
Each night I sit in the corner, on the floor, and count the men
Who go into Mama's room: 10;
And how many nurses I've met at the clinic every time Mama
Has to get stitches or other stuff: 5, just like me.

VIMBA!

The crisp of the morning is slowly melting into the midday sun.
Vimba!
The shrill bursts through the murmuring –
A grandmother's pension is a good fix for three Nyaope boys.

Truck drivers congregate in front of the Motel, waiting for their next call out.
Vimba!
A shopkeeper retrieves some stolen groceries –
The suspect loses his teeth to the pounding fists of heavyset men.

Vimba! Vimba!
A mother clutches the towel which secures a tiny infant to her back.
He skirt rips and falls to the ground as plastic bags spill tomatoes and tin fish onto the muddy street –
Her identity and dignity is stolen; an illegal immigrant is now a married citizen.

The City begins to crawl into its den and prepares to sleep with one eye open.
Vimba!
Bricks fly like pebbles, bullets ring through the air like raindrops –
A father won't make it home tonight and the shit hole claims its prize.

CROSS
ROADS

TERUGKEERING

Die branders klap nog ewe hard teen die rotse,
Nog so spierwit en skuimerig soos ek onthou.
Die skepe, steeds so geroes, sleep nog dagliks hul karige vangs
Na die hawe.

Die taxi bestuurders staan die ewe trots,
Almal werk nog by hul poste;
Onthou nog skoolsdae toe ons moes tou staan
Vir sitplekke.

En die strate lyk nog dieselfde:
Ou bure skinder nog lekker.
Geen nuwe gesiggies nie,
Net bekendes al hoe ouer.

Hoe gerieflik stap almal in hul ouers se voetspore;
Die lewe gaan maar aan.
Net kastig ek wat anders gloei;
Die Groot Stad doen mos dit aan jou.

En Oupa bly nou stoksiel alleen
Met Ouma se herinnering altyd op die tafel gedek.
Soms verskyn sy so vaagweg tussen die sonstrale
Om 'n koppie tee en 'n glimlag te deel.

Kyk hoe lê my ma se bitter woorde
Voor een en al se deurpos,
Om vining te herinner: ek's nou meer vreemdeling
As huiskind, en dis hoe mens terugkeer.

MIXED ENOUGH

They call me yellow-bone, here.
Where I grew up, I was brown-skinned,
Not that pretty;
Nice hair, at least.

They call my thighs thick, here.
Where I'm from, they never
Missed an opportunity to
Jeer at my fat fat.

I was taught to love
My grandmother's milky skin
And Irish eyes but
Not the kink in her Bushman hair.

My speech is not their crass slur
So they call me *larny*, here
There's no vernac that rolls off my tongue;
I'm the scorn they drag through their teeth

Because I look like them
But not like others,
Sound like those
They'd burn alive in the streets while the rest watch...

Even here, where I can sway
My Sarah Baartman proudly,
This Malay hair is too straight
To claim home soil.

I am a tasteful novelty
That adds spice to their social gatherings;
The anomaly that is never black black;
Just mixed enough to accommodate.

SEX AND THE CITY (Pt 2)

My sister sits on her plastic fold-up chair with her legs spread open.
She says the customers like to look before they buy – the goods must be on display.
She wears a shimmering blouse with the buttons undone, the same way our mother did, even on rainy days.
My sister is the star of the block; she's one of the pretty ones, they say.
I leave her sleeping in the morning when I go to school;
She works the night shift to pay my fees – I help her count the money in piles of 200.
We keep a moneybox hidden in the hole on the side of the couch:
Our savings for when we move from the grey building.
This has been our home for seven years –
Since Mama died, since my sister turned 15, since I was born.
My sister drinks from the bottle the way the men do.
They like her singing voice but slap her mouth if she talks too much – a woman must know her place, they say.
Some parts of her face and arms have permanent stains from the red ointment we buy from the Chinaman; the same stains I try to wash from my fingertips every morning.
But it's not all bad: some of the men smell nice, and talk nice.
My sister is teaching me to be nice, too, like Mama taught her.
When we move from this building I will have my own room
And I won't have to sit in the passage when the visitors come.
For now, my sister works the night shift and we count the money in piles of 200.

HEART LESS

There are pieces scattered throughout this body;
Mis-shapen rounds and quads, triangular ovals
With sharp, blunt edges;
Shards I've stashed in bloody corners and soft tissues –
No one is *really* brave enough to go hunting in the depths.

There are inscriptions beneath these pieces;
Engraved in ancestral tongues,
But I've scattered them throughout this body,
Hidden from ignorant eyes and blasphemous mouths –
No one is *really* open to the truth.

Neat and deliberate fortresses now lay in ruins;
The debris floating amongst defeated
Red and White Blood soldiers -
Knights in Shining Armour were quick to conquer walls
And leave their war-raging stench in the rubble.

And I have shared, willingly.
Broken off chunks and unlocked padlocks;
I've blindly guided cold hands and sly smirks
Through the shadows where my Forefathers whisper.
They have forgiven my trespasses as I do not forget those.

There's a hologram suspended amongst the remnants,
Humming a lullaby:
Be still, hidden where peace is;
You don't have to Heart anymore, there's no discovering your
pieces.
No one is *really* brave enough to go hunting in the depths.

AFRIKA KIND

Afrika-kind, hoekom steek jy so weg
Agter die wêreld se make-up en relaxers,
Elke seisoen se next-best-trend?
Waarom vlug jy van jou geboorte reg;
Hoekom is jou erfenis so sondelik,
So bitter op jou tong?

Sien jy nie hoe brom die mode
Om jou boskop hare;
Hoe smag so baie op hierdie holiday strande
Na jou goud-bruin melanien?

Maar jy, Afrika-kind, is 'n vlugteling
Van jou moedertaal.
Jy frons op jou moederland;
Jy is jou eie vyand.

Voel jy nie hoe die aarder onder jou voete
Bewe na die ritme van jou
XA... CI... QU?!
Hoe instrumente jou saligheid murmereer
As jy so TLA... KE... NGU
So MM, AA, RE, RA?!

Joune is 'n eeuw-lange gebedslied
Na ons voorvaders:
'N reëndans, 'n danksegging;
Dit wat deur die blare fluister
Wanneer die winde met die Hemel gesels.

Afrika-kind, jou oë is donker,
Jou hare 'n mengelmoes,
Jou vel uitdruklik deur die Son gesoen.

Jy is die naamgenoot van die grond waarop jy loop.
Jou hande die opsigters van al die bloedlyne
Wat die wêreld vasstel.

Maar jy, Afrika-kind... jy is steeds 'n vlugteling van jouself;
Meer bang vir jouself as dié Wat jou neerdruk.

WITCH

They call me a Witch
Because my complexion and hair texture
Doesn't allow their minds to wrap around any other –
Sangoma is a name they reserve for their kind;
Keep within the confines of names
Their tongues can twist around.
My name is too easy on the palate,
Too colonised to associate with my
Bushman blood and Khoi curves.
Witch, I am!
Because I mix and prescribe their muti
In different terms and
Burn impepho the Pagan way.

How dare I summon and channel Ancestors?
Which clan names do I call, if in the same breath
I offer praises to the four corners of the Universe
And whisper commands to its elements?
This magic that dances in the shadows
Of my candlelight invoke spirits, they say.
And when I pray I cast mesmerising spells –
I vibrate at too rapid a frequency.

So careful, this Witch may turn you into a toad.

JEPPE

The clinic is overcrowded today; more than usual – there's a crooked queue winding out the door into the yard. The chairs have lost their orderly grouping and everyone is just finding a seat wherever they can. The nurse will come out and shout about it again. Onah is tenth in line but it's obvious that she'll probably only leave around lunchtime – it's just gone 8:05am. The other women in her row are chatting away nonchalantly; they're used to this long wait. Some of them carry snacks in plastic packets; others have their bags filled with all sorts of necessities. Onah only has her ID book and some taxi money stuffed in her pockets. She wasn't sure what else to bring or how long she would have to wait. She couldn't risk going out to get *amagwinya* from the lady on the corner; she might lose her spot. Food is the last thing on her mind, anyway.

There's an old man hunched on the long bench against the wall. His body is limped over so far that his head is hanging between his legs and threatening to pull him down onto the floor. No one is helping him up or nudging him to move closer for his turn; people are taking advantage of the opportunity to take a seat ahead of him. A loud cough from somewhere in the large room startles him and he shifts his heaviness into an almost upright position. His face is frail; the grey thickets of brows hanging above his eyes make him look like an old dog. He is wheezing severely, clutching the small, brown pouch where his wrinkling documents are tucked in. The woman sitting next to him leans over and whispers something urgent to him while pointing at the little boy playing by her feet. The old man musters a broken smile and nods. She moves ahead of him and turns her back without a thank you. His head is dropping again; his shoulders heaving heavier.

Thirty minutes have passed and the line of patients waiting outside the toilets hasn't moved at all. Two nurses have rushed in there and their agitated orders are barely audible over the horrific wailing coming from inside. A woman is screaming; her husband is shouting about incompetence. The matron is barking authoritative threats. The staff restroom has now become a unisex facility as the nurses try and diffuse the frantic situation. There are more angry patients than curious; no one cares why the woman is in such agony. Her trauma is not their problem – she is holding up the line. A nurse emerges from the room carrying a beaker with a bloody urine sample. The woman is motioned to take a seat in another section. No one is moved by her sobbing; her test results are not more urgent than anyone else's.

"Next?!" An impatient call bellows from the small room where patients have been entering and exiting for the better part of the morning. A busty nurse sits behind the cluttered desk. She mumbles a greeting but doesn't look up. Her movements are second-nature; years of routine: roll up sleeves, read blood pressure; swab and prick finger, drop blood on test plate; scribble results on card, dismiss patient to next room. Several nurses barge into the room to chat about random things. They don't seem to care that someone is perched nervously on a chair waiting for life-changing news. Their judgemental glares and snide remarks are inconsistent with what a caregiver should be. "Where is your husband? Don't they teach you about condoms in school? It's not my problem; I'm going to lunch now." Their combined energies bounce off the walls and make the room even colder. Everyone leaving the room looks even sicker when coming out than when they went in.

Onah drags her numb body to its feet and shuffles into the examining room. The hours of sitting down have caused pins and needles all through her limbs and she shifts anxiously in her chair. The routine begins; Onah has questions but the nurse isn't interested. She can barely understand the hurried explanations that the sister is rattling off: the blood test is for- this injection is for- take two of these; one of these- don't drink... Her heart is racing. How is she going to remember all of this? There's no one who will remind her or make sure every day goes according to schedule. The nurse is staring at Onah with an expectant frown; she is waiting for a response... Onah walks to the gate clutching the four bags of pills wrapped in her jersey – she thought it would only be Calcium and Iron tablets. That's what her friend told her. She remembers to buy two *'magwinya*; one for her hunger and one for the growing foetus. She clutches her jersey tighter while walking to the taxi stop: Antiretrovirals and some other brown ones: now that's a hard pill to swallow.

LAST STRAW

Aunt Miriam came running towards our rusted gate.
Mama hurried her inside, as she usually did –
Wiping camphor and savlon-soaked cotton over her swollen face.
Aunt Miriam was dripping blood all over the kitchen tiles;
She had no more finger nails.

"You'll help me with the funeral arrangements?"
She asked-told Mama...

They hugged as the police sirens came closer.

LETTING GO

Old leaves are easily shaken when
Strong winds blow;
And often they do fall.
Though cling with their every might and all,
The branch knows best to let them go.

FULL STEAM AHEAD

SURVIVING

I survive in the cells
Which seek no taming.

Here, there are no scabs
To pick at, no

Old festering wounds.
I am regenerating, insistently,

Persistently surviving.

INSTRUCTIONS FOR CHAOS

Wear a hat
Wear suspenders
Wear underpants, or not
And show your bra straps
Wear loafers
Wear a neck tie
Wake up and go out
And show off your messy hair
Wear your cap back-to-front
Wear sneakers with a dress
Go to bed with no shirt on
And adjust your underwear in public, shamelessly

By any means necessary:
Be you
Be whimsical
Seek inner peace
Be brave
Be a rebel
Speak fearlessly

Build empires
Spoil yourself
Never mind a pants-suit -
Bulldoze boardrooms in a doek
And pumps

Chase financial freedom
Kiss passionately
Love deeply and unconditionally
Support artists
Buy books
Invest
Laugh deliriously

Smell delicious
Taste addictively

A GOOD WIFE

In my country, when a baby dies, the mother is not allowed at the funeral or burial grounds. I think she is not even allowed to know the exact location where her child's body was laid to rest. They say it's supposed to give her some sort of comfort... comfort, in not knowing?

My grandfather taught us that in our culture we wear white to a funeral service or a wake. My grandmother had a different belief and always scoffed at his "superstitions". She wore white all the time, much to her husband's disdain. She taught me well how to be a rebel. When she died, I wore the pale blue kaftan she had knitted for my 21st birthday. I was the talk of the village for more than a month.

My family accepted the offer to marry, on my behalf, soon after I turned 22 and I was bargained off to South Africa faster than I could protest. My husband was a taxi driver in Hillbrow – so he said – and promised me luxury and comfort. Hillbrow sounded posh and English; I didn't know any better, I didn't know anything about this City of Gold. My mother gave me a list of do's and don'ts: rules that a good wife should abide by to keep her husband happy. I only heard my grandmother's island slur in my head: *ya nobuddy's doormat, ya hear?*

I spent my days cooking and cleaning our small apartment – my husband liked things just so. My groceries were bought at the *spaza* across the street or another discount Super just one block from our building; I never ventured any further. From our window on the 7th floor, I would sit and watch the men shake hands and exchange boisterous conversation; there were rows of women in front of a salon braiding hair; I'd witness the occasional swap of weed for money – sometimes small white packets. The cars and taxis and trucks were always loud; the Vimba's even louder. I had no business going out there, no way. I waited patiently, every day, for my husband to return from work with his daily takings and a flower.

Two years had passed and my inlaws had grown tired of waiting for a grandchild. After months of snide remarks and awkward silences, they demanded that my husband find a second wife. I was deemed useless and not worth of my *lobola*. I knew it was the beginning of the end. My husband no longer came home from work and when he did, he reeked of beer and sex. We didn't talk anymore. If our walls could talk they'd only mention the frightening death threats and muffled grunts when he raped me. I was a good wife, the way my mother instructed me to be. My silent obedience was his reward.

I woke up one morning and realised that my husband had not been home in almost a month. I had managed to make a few pennies by selling sweets and crotchet items to the women in the building. The landlord had been kind enough to ignore the late rent, as long as he could visit for supper, now and then. Because my husband was no longer around, I had to brave the rowdy streets and quickly learned how to duck and dive my way around town to find bargains and clients and more often than not, food. Everything came at a price, especially for a dark-skinned *kwerekwere* like me.

One month turned into two, turned into seven. My belly was expanding and I could no longer ignore the growing being that kicked and turned every night. I had read that you could find the best medical care at the hospitals here, at least better than my rural village clinic. There were countless other women from my country around the area; they all had two and three babies. Mine would be fine, too.

It was freezing on the morning I went into labour. I had managed to limp all the way from our street to the Hillbrow hospital where I had to wait in a queue with other labouring mothers. *There are no open beds,* the sister yelled through the corridor.

When they eventually wheeled my exhausted, bloody body into the general ward, I was the only non-South African there, hidden behind the white curtains. My baby wouldn't make it through the night, they said. It was too small and too underdeveloped. I could go home in the morning.

I stood by the gate, holding the small box that the nurses had given to me when I left the ward. Across the street was a blue door; I knew very well where it led and walked over with my box. I dragged my tender legs up the seven flights of stairs and placed the box on the altar by the Medicine Man's door. There was no need to wait, no need to know... life had to move on, and the white dress the nurses had given me had to be burned.

RUNAWAY TRAIN

the room is spinning;
perhaps it's the bed... or my racing thoughts

the nurse is casual;
she's not the one who will be gutted open

my legs are numbing;
i can't run away anymore, can't change my mind

it's happening now.

there are hands probing
instruments snipping
they tell me to relax

hours of waiting
turn into minutes of pushing and pulling
one last tug, one snip of the chord

it's over now.

a tiny voice is screaming;
the room is filled with joyful cheers

tears are involuntarily rolling;
did I do it or did they

i'm holding my reward;
he is all of heaven; I am slowly slipping into a new hell

it's only the beginning now.

STAYING ABREAST OF THINGS

They were never really round:
Some sort of melon-shaped.
I've only ever known them as huge.
There were no tiny mounds and
Perky browns pitching miniature tents
Inside my shirts – always just been
BREASTS!
They've been the object of self-loathing;
Two sacks I wished I could amputate.
They've served as eye candy to
Gawking teenage boys and old pervs alike –
Boobs, Tits, Nana's!
Then they became toys to play with:
Fond things to fondle in affection, passion;
To misuse, abuse –
Tata's, Jugs, Hooters!
Girly... womanly... now motherly:
Swollen, tight; no suitable bra to contain them.
Itchy, cracked; I'm supposed to feed a person with these?
Brown, then red, then black as hell...
Black?!
Breast is best, they keep telling me,
So I sit up all night with a little mouth
Sucking profusely at black nipples,
Cracked nipples where milk only trickles –
Suck, suck! Drink, eat!
No nourishment for a helpless little mouth.
Bigger, rounder, heavier;
Stretch marks covering stretched marks: emptier.
But breast is best, they keep telling me
As crying eyes beg with an open mouth
For Boobs, Titties, Breasts
That will eventually go back to being
Two, sort of melon-shaped bags to be

Gawked at, fondled, and perhaps again
Try to be food.

JOURNEY

BiRth marks,
S t r e t c h marks,
Beauty spots;
Camouflage birth SCARS,
Years
Passed...
Wrinkly parts.

HOLDING ON

There are dried petals on the floor, in the dust.
In the corners, spider webs collect the sun's rays
And turn them into shadows.
On the windowsill, a glass case cracks:
Between the thorns, new leaves begin to grow.

Dewdrops capture moonshine from midnight's glow
To offer a sacrifice to the morning Sun.
Sleeping buds lift their humbled bow
To salute the rising halo.
Shadows return to their slumber and
Make way for new love –
The morning is for giving;
The morning is forgiving.

GOOD FATHERS

Let it never go unwritten,
the truth about good men.

May this generation and those to come
know that good fathers nurtured them.

Teach our daughters that
not every man is a dog;

For there are jewels scattered
amongst us, who mimic gods!

MASTER CHEF

Important: follow all instructions methodically to achieve the best results.
Ingredients will yield a lifetime supply of magic.

take 10 tiny fingers
10 twinkle toes
hold tightly while rocking
a few ounces of cuddly love
add 2 sparkling eyes
a little pinch of nose, 2 pouty lips
kiss gently until giggles fill
the air

LESEDI

Last night I dreamt I swallowed a shooting star.

It was neither yellow nor orange,

But it was fiery

And turned my skies to gold!

EPILOGUE

Johannesburg: a vibrant, bustling, diverse, energetic, filthy, heavy place. These streets are both beautiful and ugly at the same time. It's interesting how you can love something and also hate it, in one breath. I could be anywhere in the world right now but there's no place I'd rather be... right now.

Joburg teaches you more about yourself than you'd ever learn elsewhere in South Africa, I think. This is a place where patience and tolerance is tested to its wits end on the daily. People walk as they please; cars are driven carelessly; and taxis... oh, taxis are something else! Nothing and no one gives way because everything and everyone are on their own way. There's very little courtesy here, almost no sympathy – but there's still something mysteriously magical about here.

I didn't think I would come to love Joburg. My first year in this place was so sheltered and painful. I knew only the walls of our house in the West Rand and nothing else. Ruimsig: red sand, white people, racist dogs, silence... far from everything! I didn't mind it at first, but it wasn't *Joburg*. I experienced nothing, and eventually despised it. I'm glad that chapter ended as abruptly as it did. The horrors of my time there haunted me for a long time, sometimes still visit my dreams, but they're distant memories now. Memories I can often laugh at when they try to taunt me.

I'm not sure why I love Jozi. Why would anyone love the stench and the filth and the crowds? Why would anyone love so much crime and scowl? Indifference and prejudice thrives here, after all: brother hates brother and sister have no compassion for sister... But I have *found* myself here. Among the chaos, I feel more alive and hopeful here. PE could never do this for me. Home was never where the heart is; it was a slow death.

Johannesburg is not exactly home, either. At most, I might even say I feel like a foreigner who has come to seek refuge or exile here for a period; a refugee in my own country – at home, still displaced. I have experienced some of my best and worst times in this place. Stared at because I look different, talk differently, act differently. I've been shunned, insulted, welcomed and accepted; often in one meeting. This is not a city for the faint-hearted, I tell you. I admit, there are times I've felt I would not make it here, that I would literally wither away: emotionally at first; psychologically would follow quickly after, and then physically I would perish from elements beyond my control (self-harm looked very attractive on most days).

But I made it! I survived and still survive through dire odds. In Johannesburg: the city of golden, cracked dreams that could come true if you really want it to...

ABOUT THE AUTHOR

Flow Wellington – government name, Selome Payne – grew up in Port Elizabeth. Sources confirm that she was born in Johannesburg; which may explain why the city has always called to her.

She began writing at the age of 12 and has since published in numerous international and local anthologies. At some point in her life, she was a prominent (curvy) figure and active participant in the Eastern Cape poetry and hip hop scene, featuring on True Sight Music's 2009 mixtape, which was nominated for a Hype award (it had to be mentioned!).

Flow is the founding owner of Poetree Publications, a self-publishing institute which assists writers from the African continent (and sometimes bleeding-heart foreigners) to publish their work. The company has, since its establishment in 2011, published 15 different projects including her own collections: The Undelivered Score (2011) and Gau-Trained (2018). A win for the Coloureds, yes!

Flow lives in Johannesburg with her partner and son and only comes out of hiding if the price is right ☺.

Social Media links:
Facebook: Poetree Publications
Twitter: @PoetreeBooks
Instagram: @the_poetree

Citiations:
* *The City* – also published in Women Poets: Within & Beyond Shores, Vol II 2017 (compiled by Dr Shamenaz Bano, Allahabad)
* *Where I'm From* – also published in To Breathe Into Another Voice, a South African Jazz Anthology (Edited by Myesha Jenkins) & Absolute Africa (anthology compiled by Patricia Schonstein)
* *Staying Abreast of Things* – also published in The Atlanta Review 2017 (edited by Phillippa Yaa De Villiers)

Poetree Publications (Pty) Ltd
K2015341299
2015/341299/07

www.ingramcontent.com/pod-product-compliance
Lightning Source LLC
LaVergne TN
LVHW041237150826
845673LV00008B/2410

* 9 7 8 0 9 9 4 6 9 5 0 2 4 *